EXTREME SCIENCE EXPLORERS

EXPLORE THE CENTER OF THE EARTH

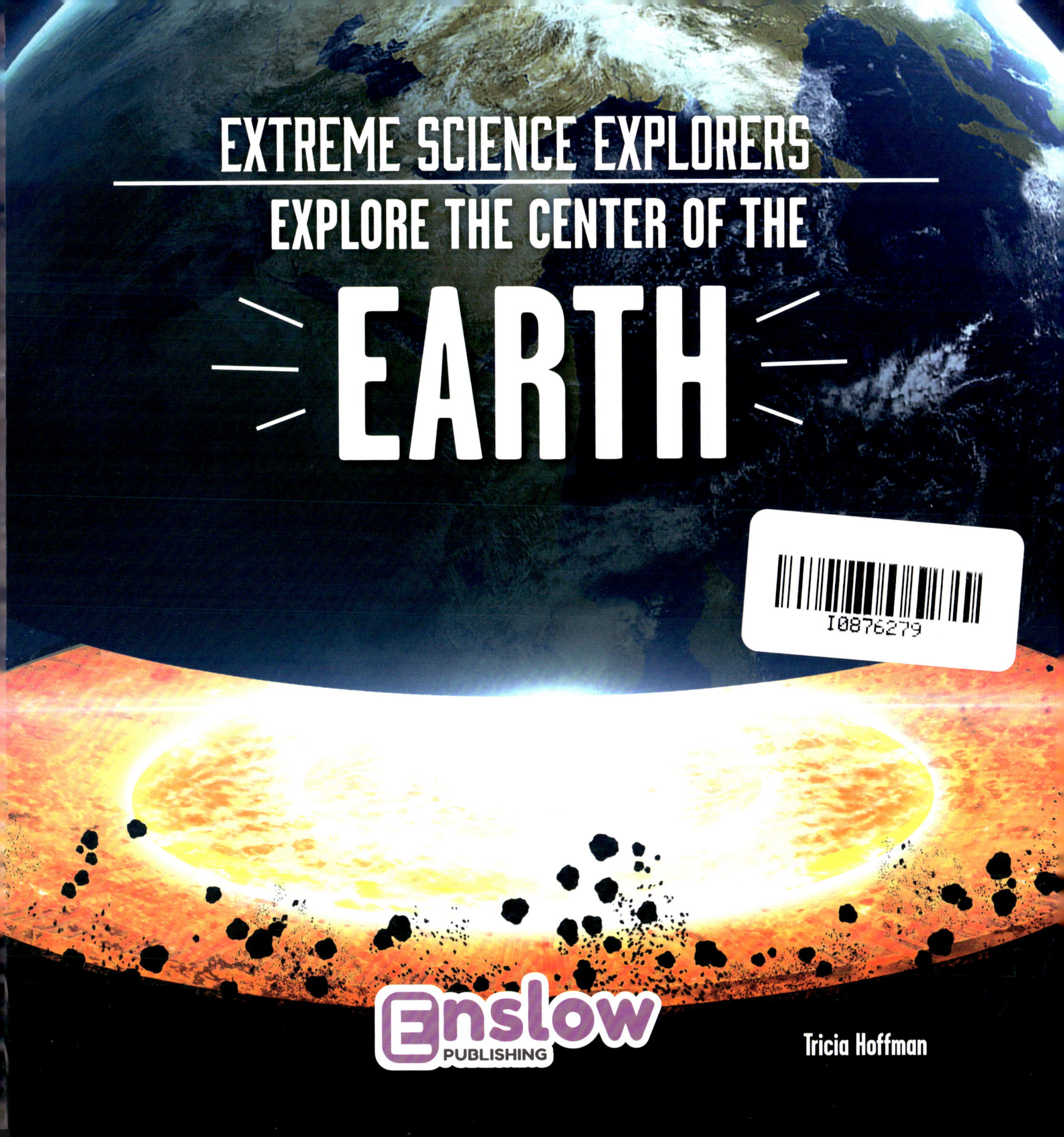

Enslow PUBLISHING

Tricia Hoffman

Please visit our website, www.enslow.com. For a free color catalog of all our high-quality books, call toll free 1-800-398-2504 or fax 1-877-980-4454

Published in 2027 by
Enslow Publishing
2544 Clinton Street
Buffalo, NY 14224

Portions of this work were originally authored by Janey Levy and published as *Fantastic Science Journeys: A Trip to the Center of the Earth*. All new material in this edition is authored by Tricia Hoffman.

Cataloging-in-Publication Data
Names: Hoffman, Tricia.
Title: Explore the center of the Earth / Tricia Hoffman.
Description: Buffalo, NY : Enslow Publishing, 2027. | Series: Extreme science explorers | Includes glossary and index.
Identifiers: ISBN 9781978548961 (pbk.) | ISBN 9781978548978 (library bound) | ISBN 9781978548985 (ebook)
Subjects: LCSH: Earth (Planet)--Internal structure--Juvenile literature. | Earth (Planet)--Core--Juvenile literature. | Earth (Planet)--Mantle--Juvenile literature. | Earth (Planet)--Crust--Juvenile literature.
Classification: LCC QE509.H644 2027 | DDC 551.112--dc23

Printed in China

Photos Credits: Cover, p. 1 Vadim Sadovski/Shutterstock.com; p. 3 Mr.SunThree/Shutterstock.com; p. 4 Photoongraphy/Shutterstock.com; p. 4 Risto Raunio/Shutterstock.com; p. 6 Labunskiy Konstantin/Shutterstock.com; p. 8 Nicholas Courtney/Shutterstock.com; p. 8 papa papong/Shutterstock.com; p. 10 Mistervlad/Shutterstock.com; p. 11 Adwo/Shutterstock.com; p. 12 jarino/Shutterstock.com; p. 16 Ellen Bronstayn/Shutterstock.com; p. 16 Scandphoto/Shutterstock.com; p. 18 Andrii Duhin/Shutterstock.com; p. 22 Nordroden/Shutterstock.com; p. 24 oliverdelahaye/Shutterstock.com; p. 27 Pixabay/Wiki; p. 28 Danielle W Press/Shutterstock.com; p. 14, 20 Skshoot/Shutterstock.com

CPSIA compliance information: Batch #QSENS27: For further information, contact Enslow Publishing, New York, New York, at 1-800-398-2504.

TABLE OF CONTENTS

JOURNEY FAR BELOW

The inside of planet Earth is an extreme place. What if you could travel all the way down to its center? You'd need to push through **layers** of hard rock and into molten lava. This is something that no one has ever done before.

French writer Jules Verne imagined a trip to Earth's center in his famous 1864 book *A Journey to the Center of the Earth*. Verne imagined giant caves, rivers, and creatures from the age of dinosaurs inside Earth. But as you're about to see, the center of the planet is nothing like that!

As you travel down, it gets very hot very quickly. The **pressure** becomes extreme. It's going to be a wild ride. So get ready to dig deep. Let's explore!

THAT'S EXTREME!

Earth looks blue from space because water covers more than 70 percent of the surface.

Earth's oceans hold about 96.5 percent of all water. But the ocean's water is full of salt, so we can't drink it.

Mountains are formed in the lithosphere, which is the outermost physical layer.

WHAT'S INSIDE EARTH?

Earth is not a solid sphere. Its **interior** is divided into layers. Scientists often talk about the layers in terms of their composition, or what matter they're made of. There are three compositional layers. Think of Earth like the inside of a cherry, with a thin outer layer, a thick middle layer, and a solid center.

Scientists also separate Earth's interior into layers based on **physical** properties. This is how the matter acts. Earth has five physical layers.

THAT'S EXTREME!

Earth's layers aren't completely separate. They interact with each other all the time by exchanging heat and materials in a cycle. This shapes everything on Earth, from continents to climate.

COMPOSITIONAL LAYERS

Earth's compositional layers are the crust, mantle, and core. The crust is the outermost layer, as well as the thinnest. It is the surface on which we live! It consists of rocks made mostly of **silica**.

Underneath the crust is the mantle. The mantle is the largest layer. It makes up more than 80 percent of Earth! The mantle is made of silica, iron, and magnesium.

And finally, at the center of Earth, is the core. The core can be represented by the pit of the cherry. It is made of liquid iron and nickel, as well as oxygen and sulfur.

THAT'S EXTREME!

Since no one has actually made a trip to the center of Earth, how do we know about the layers? Scientists have learned about them by measuring how waves created by ***earthquakes*** *travel through Earth.*

The crust is thickest under mountains. It is up to 28 miles (45 km) thick around the Rocky Mountains in Colorado.

How hard is granite? It's hard enough to scratch glass. Ancient Egyptians used it to cut statues that have survived for 4,000 years.

CREATING THE CRUST

Earth's surface is covered by the crust. Earth has two types of crust: the continental crust and the oceanic crust.

The continental crust is what you see on land. It supports the major landmasses and is 19 to 44 miles (30 to 70 km) thick. It's mostly made of silica in the form of extremely hard rock called granite. It is older and thicker than oceanic crust.

Oceanic crust is the crust found under the oceans. It is younger and thinner than continental crust. It's only 3 to 6 miles (5 to 10 km) thick. But it's **denser**. It's made mostly of hard rock called basalt. The oceanic crust has less silica and more iron and magnesium than the continental crust.

THAT'S EXTREME!

Basalts are "sima" rocks. Sima stands for "silicate and magnesium," which are the most abundant minerals in oceanic crust.

OCEANIC CRUST

Oceanic crust is constantly forming. It forms where the seafloor spreads at mid-ocean ridges. Mid-ocean ridges are underwater mountain ranges formed by the movement of tectonic (tehk-TAH-nihk) plates. As the plates spread and separate, magma from Earth's mantle rises to fill the gap. The magma cools and solidifies, creating new oceanic crust!

To get to the center of Earth, we must first tunnel through the crust. The oceanic crust may be thinner, but it's denser and harder to reach.

On the coast of North America, the crust is about 19 miles (30 km) thick. That may sound like a lot of rock to travel through, but compared to other layers, it's pretty thin! Overall, the crust is the thinnest layer of Earth. It makes up less than 1 percent of Earth's mass.

THAT'S EXTREME!

The crust is broken into pieces called tectonic plates. These plates move continuously, but so slowly you don't notice it. They move more slowly than your fingernails grow!

The Grand Canyon in Arizona is about a mile (1.6 km) deep. The crust is about 18 times deeper!

FEELING HOT!

Imagine the surface temperature of Earth is a comfortable 70 degrees Fahrenheit (21 degrees Celsius). The surface pressure, called air pressure, is 14.7 pounds per square inch (1 kg per sq cm).

But remember, temperature and pressure increase as you go deeper. At the bottom of the crust, the temperature will be about 800 degrees Fahrenheit (427 degrees Celsius). That's hot enough to melt lead! The rock above you will create a pressure of about 183,750 pounds per square inch (12,500 kg per sq cm). That's enough to easily squash the strongest **submarine**.

THAT'S EXTREME!

A submarine named Deepsea Challenger was built to go deeper in the ocean and to withstand greater pressure than any other submarine. Still, it can only go 6 miles (11 km) deep.

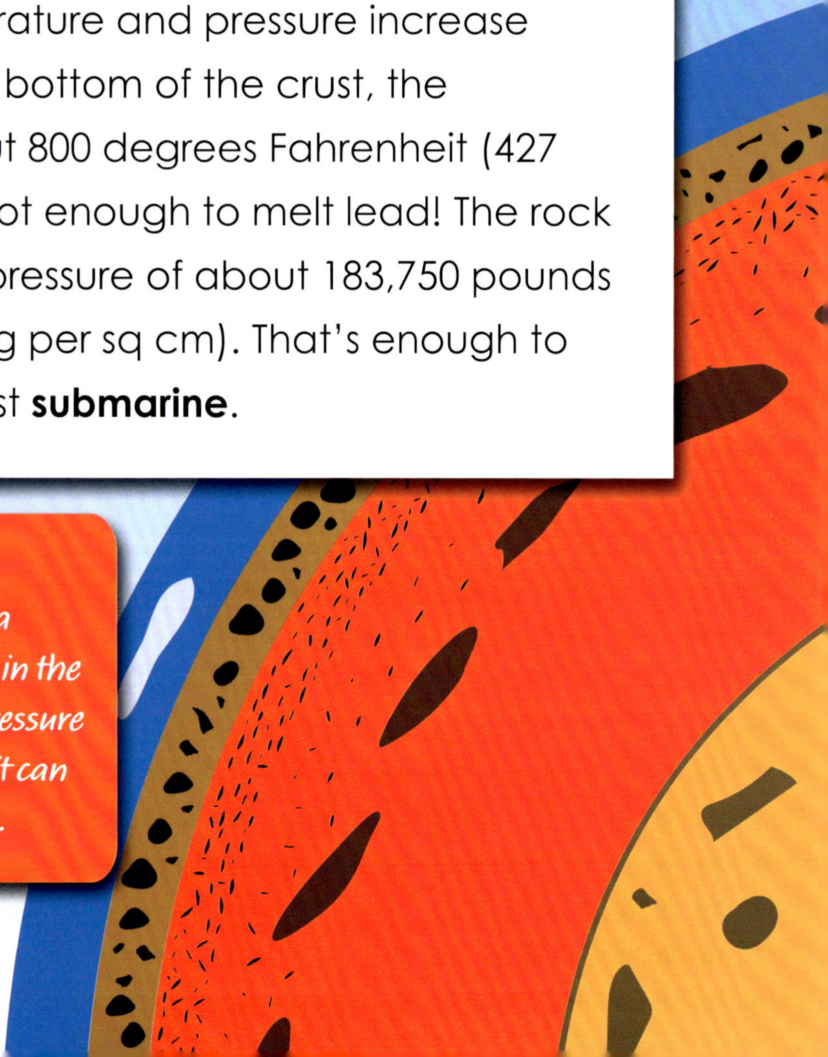

At the bottom of the crust, a border separates the crust from the mantle. It's called the Mohorovicic (maw-hawr-aw-VEE-cheech) ***discontinuity***, or "Moho" for short.

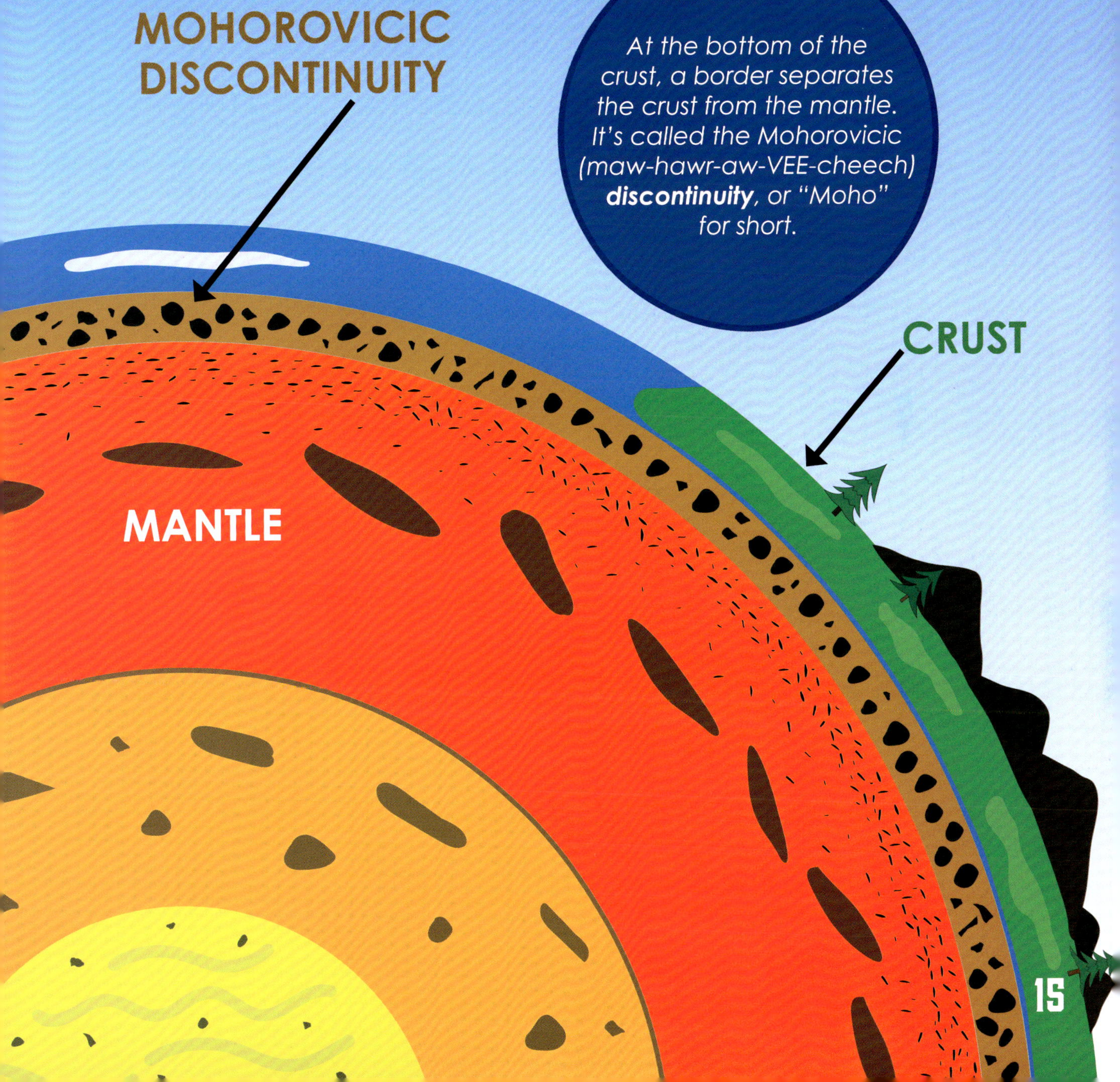

The mantle is darker and denser than the crust. That's because it's made of a rock called peridotite and includes more iron and magnesium.

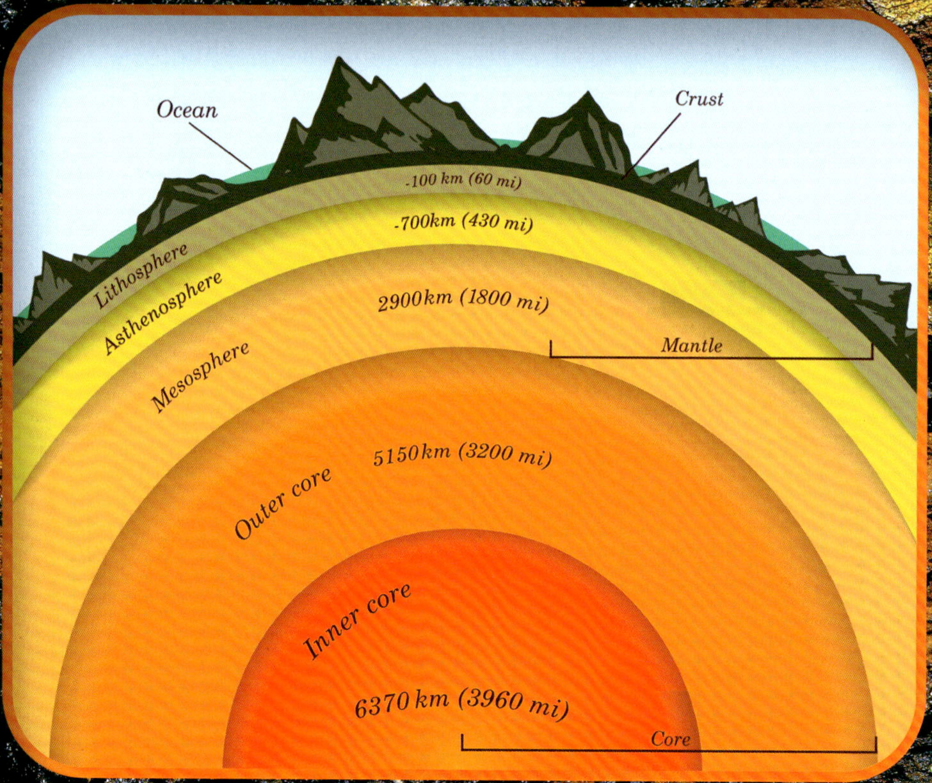

FROM THE CRUST TO THE MANTLE

After tunneling through the crust, we enter the mantle. It feels much like traveling through the crust did. That's because the uppermost part of the mantle is stiff rock that can break, just like the crust. Together, the two form what's called the lithosphere. The lithosphere is a tough shell broken into tectonic plates that float on the softer asthenosphere beneath.

By the time you reach the bottom of the lithosphere, you'll be about 93 miles (150 km) below the surface. That's 86 miles (138 km) deeper than the deepest part of the ocean!

THAT'S EXTREME!

Earth's physical layers are the lithosphere, asthenosphere, mesosphere, outer core, and inner core. We'll explore each of these layers as we go deeper inside Earth.

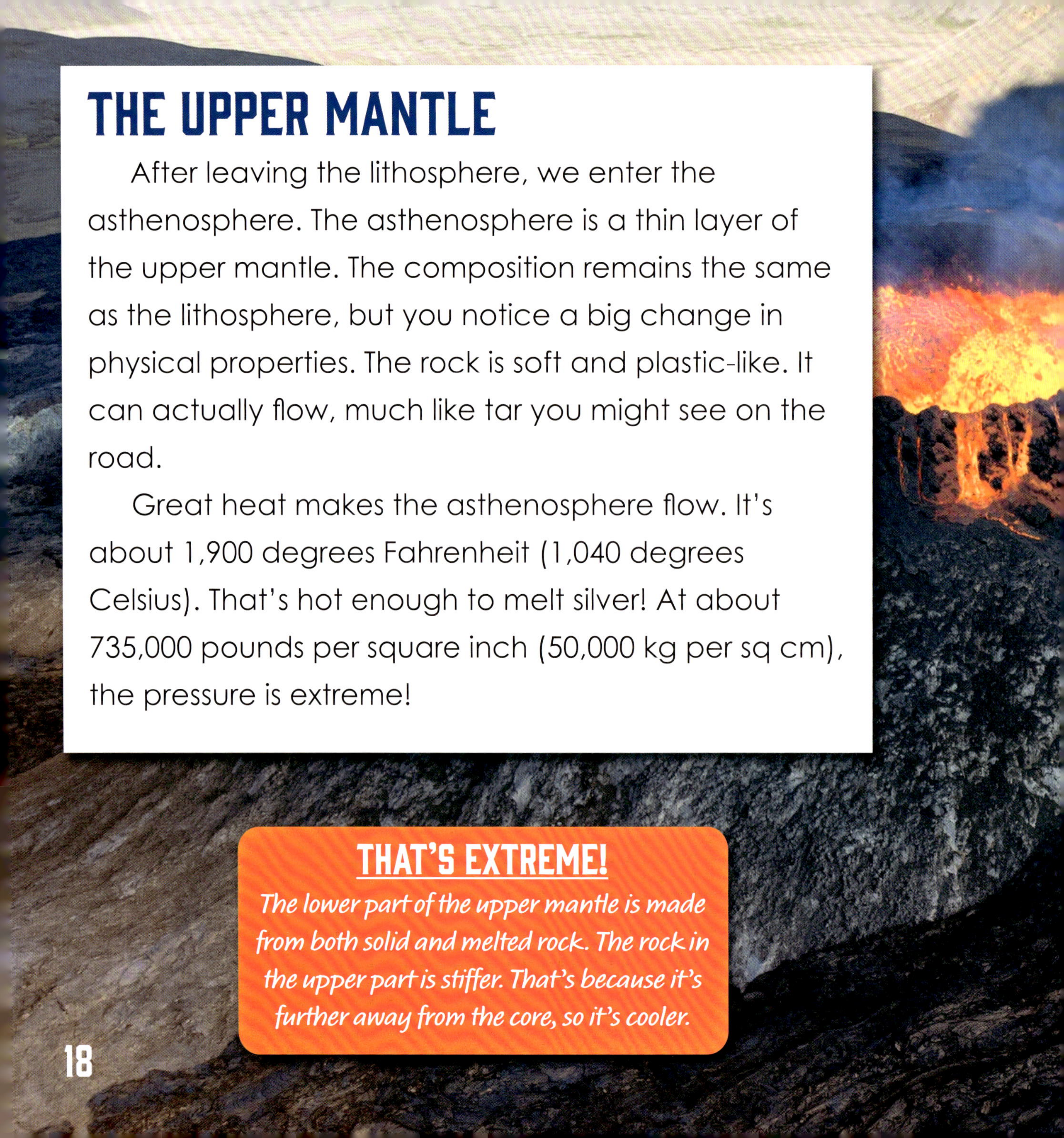

THE UPPER MANTLE

After leaving the lithosphere, we enter the asthenosphere. The asthenosphere is a thin layer of the upper mantle. The composition remains the same as the lithosphere, but you notice a big change in physical properties. The rock is soft and plastic-like. It can actually flow, much like tar you might see on the road.

Great heat makes the asthenosphere flow. It's about 1,900 degrees Fahrenheit (1,040 degrees Celsius). That's hot enough to melt silver! At about 735,000 pounds per square inch (50,000 kg per sq cm), the pressure is extreme!

THAT'S EXTREME!

The lower part of the upper mantle is made from both solid and melted rock. The rock in the upper part is stiffer. That's because it's further away from the core, so it's cooler.

The lava that comes out of ***volcanoes*** comes from the asthenosphere. That's how hot it is!

GOING LOWER

Below the asthenosphere is the lower mantle, or mesosphere. It's even hotter now—about 3,630 degrees Fahrenheit (2,000 degrees Celsius). That's hot enough to melt iron!

But even though it's so hot, the mesosphere is stiffer than the asthenosphere. That's because the pressure is so great. It's 1.4 million times the pressure on Earth's surface!

At the bottom of the mantle, there is a border separating it from the core. That border is called the Gutenberg discontinuity. It separates the solid mantle from the liquid core.

THAT'S EXTREME!

Altogether, the parts of the mantle make up about 66 percent of Earth's mass. That's more than 66 times what the crust makes up!

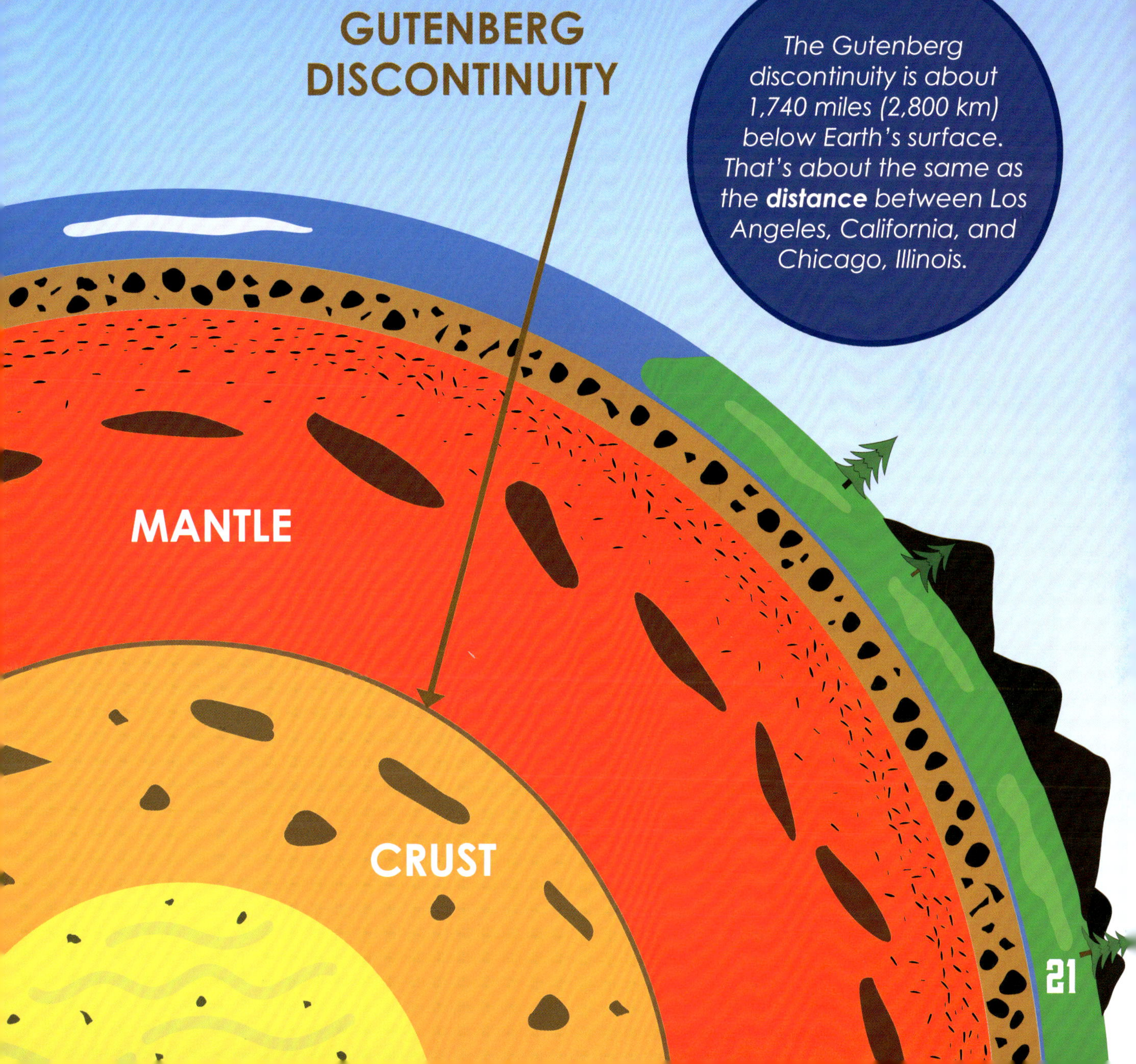

The Gutenberg discontinuity is about 1,740 miles (2,800 km) below Earth's surface. That's about the same as the **distance** between Los Angeles, California, and Chicago, Illinois.

GETTING TO THE CORE

Now, we're in the outer core. Immediately, you notice a huge difference. The outer core is liquid! How is that possible? It's because of the extreme heat.

The temperature is about 9,000 degrees Fahrenheit (5,000 degrees Celsius). Imagine how it feels on a hot, 90-degree Fahrenheit (32-degree Celsius) summer day. The outer core is 100 times hotter! The composition of the outer core also differs from that of the mantle. It's made mostly of liquid iron and nickel.

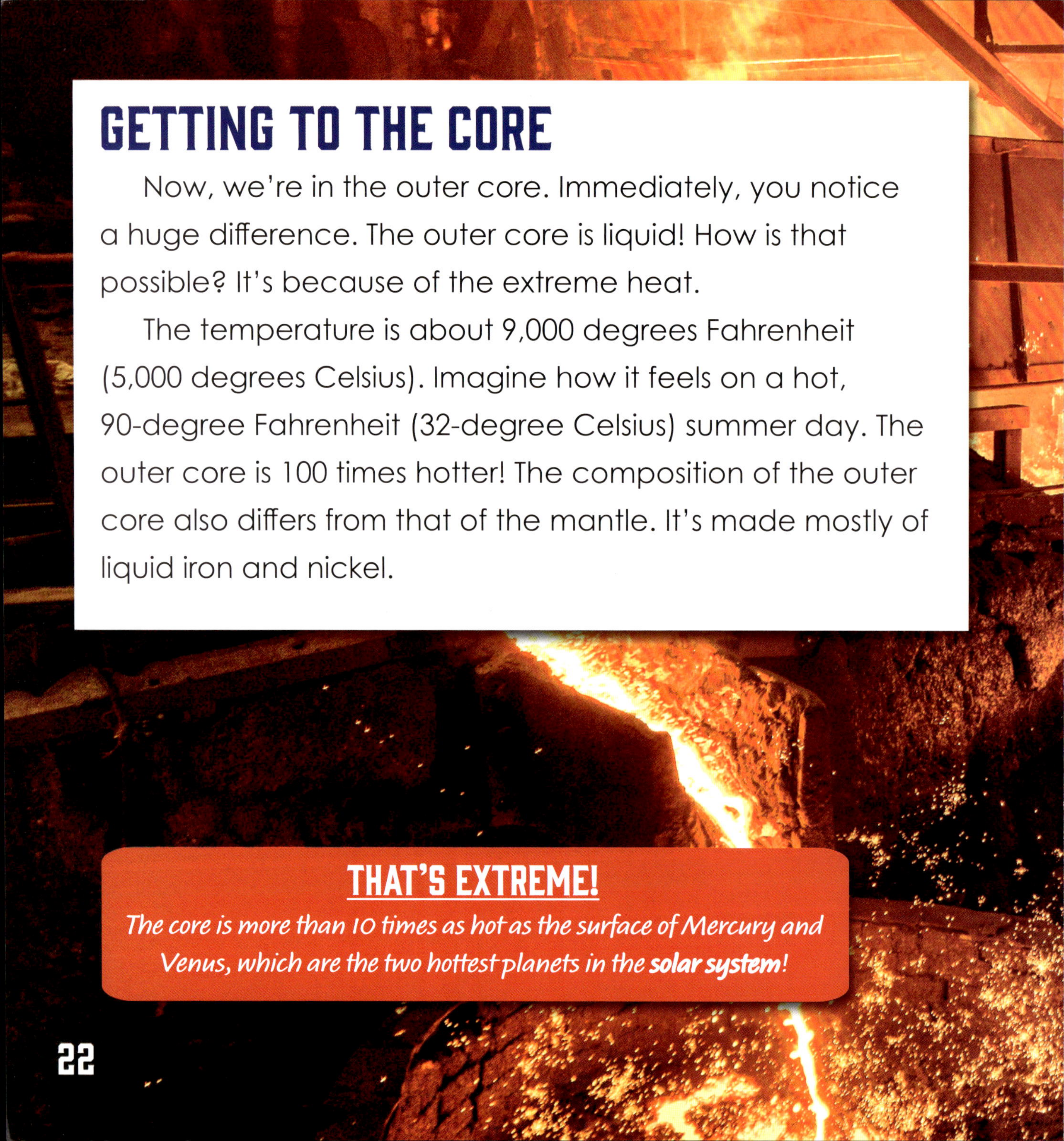

THAT'S EXTREME!

The core is more than 10 times as hot as the surface of Mercury and Venus, which are the two hottest planets in the ***solar system****!*

The outer core might look a bit like the hot, liquid iron in a factory.

The core may be deep inside Earth, but it was the first part of Earth's interior that scientists discovered. Geologist Richard Dixon Oldham found it in 1906 by studying earthquake records.

THE OUTER CORE

The hot, liquid iron of the outer core is in constant motion. It's about 1,400 miles (2,250 km) thick—that's about the distance between New York City, New York, and Austin, Texas!

Finally, you reach the bottom of the outer core. Here, the temperature is about 10,800 degrees Fahrenheit (6,000 degrees Celsius). That's as hot as the surface of the sun! And the pressure is almost unimaginable. It's about 3.3 million times what it is on Earth's surface. Humans would never survive here.

THAT'S EXTREME!

The motion of the liquid iron outer core is what creates Earth's magnetic field. The magnetic field keeps Earth safe from harmful rays that come from space.

THE CENTER OF EARTH

After passing through the outer core, we enter the very center of Earth. Earth's ball-shaped inner core is the very hot, very dense center of our planet.

The inner core's composition matches the outer core, but everything else has changed. It is the hottest part of Earth's interior, with temperatures up to 12,600 degrees Fahrenheit (7,000 degrees Celsius). Despite this, it's solid, not liquid like the outer core. Why? It's because of the extreme pressure.

Earth's core is important for understanding how our world works. Even though it's so far away, the core impacts all of life on Earth's surface.

THAT'S EXTREME!

The outer and inner cores rotate, or spin, in opposite directions. The outer core rotates toward the west, the inner core toward the east.

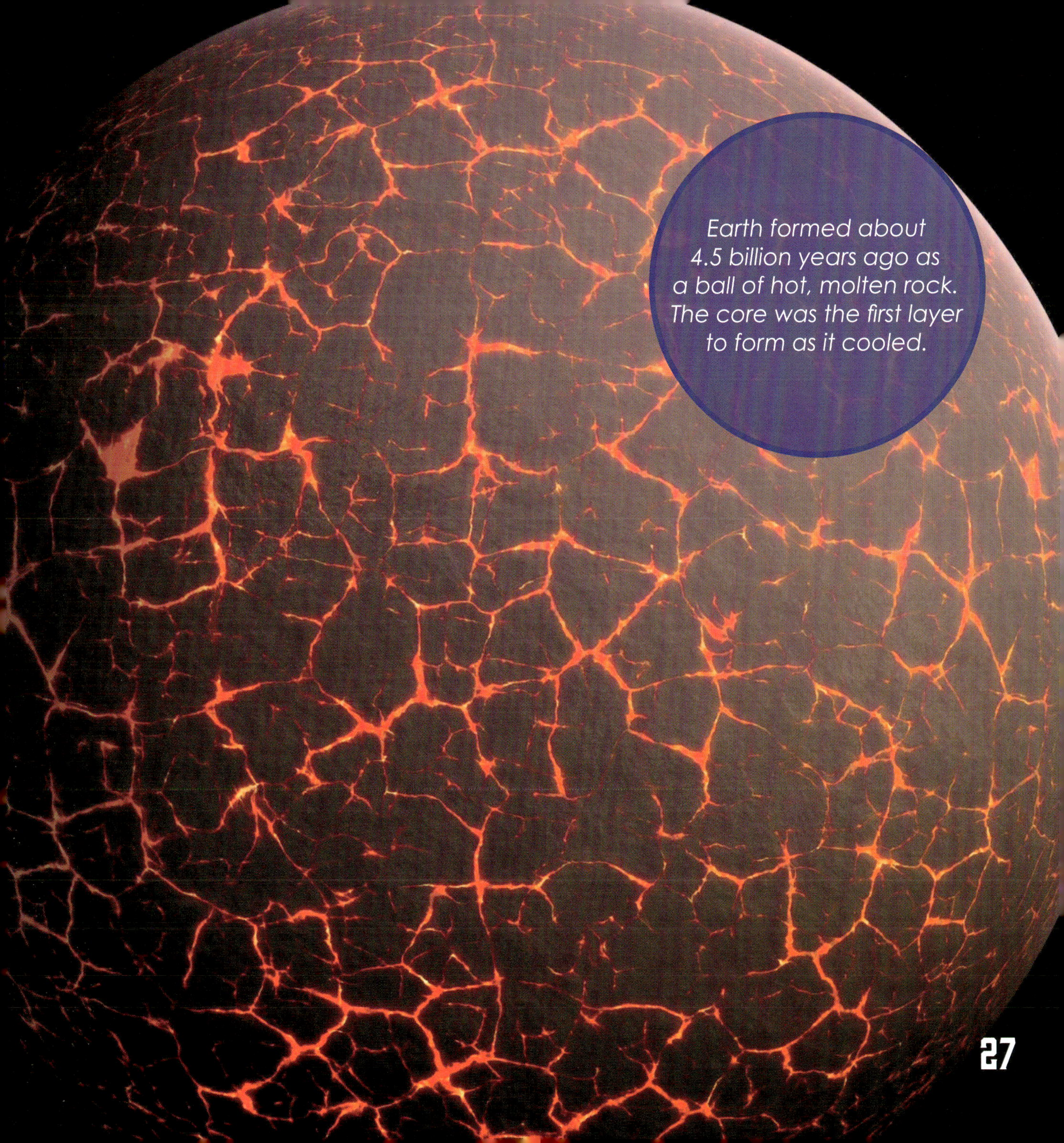

Earth formed about 4.5 billion years ago as a ball of hot, molten rock. The core was the first layer to form as it cooled.

The next time you walk along Earth's crust, imagine everything that is way down deep underneath your feet.

THE JOURNEY IS COMPLETE

You've made it! You've reached the inner core and the center of planet Earth. You've seen Earth as no one has ever seen it before.

It's nothing like the world Jules Verne imagined so long ago, but it's just as wonderful. It has solid, stiff rock; soft, plastic rock; rock so hot it's liquid; and superhot rock under such great pressure it can't melt. It's an amazing place!

THAT'S EXTREME!

It's about 3,960 miles (6,370 km) from Earth's surface to the center. That's about the same as the distance from New York City, New York, to Berlin, Germany.

GLOSSARY

dense: packed very closely together

discontinuity: a change or break in something

distance: the amount of separation between two points

earthquake: a shaking of the ground caused by the movement of Earth's crust

interior: inside

layer: one thickness of something lying over or under another

physical: having to do with natural science

pressure: a force that pushes on something else

silica: the hard matter that makes up quartz and sand

solar system: the sun and all the space objects that orbit it, including the planets and their moons

submarine: a ship built to operate underwater

volcano: an opening in a planet's surface through which hot, liquid rock sometimes flows

MORE INFORMATION

BOOKS

Baumann, Anne-Sophie. *The Ultimate Book of Planet Earth.* San Francisco, CA: Twirl, 2019.

Chartwell Books. *Inside Out Earth: Look Inside (and Outside) Our Amazing Planet.* New York, NY: Chartwell Books, 2024.

Turner, Tracey. *Up and Down: Blast up to Space or Flip this book to Dig Down to the Earth's Core!* New York, NY: Kingfisher, 2025.

WEBSITES

Earth: A Primer on the Third Rock From the Sun
https://science.howstuffworks.com/earth.htm
Learn all about Earth, find helpful diagrams, and see some amazing photos.

Structure of the Earth!
www.natgeokids.com/uk/discover/geography/physical-geography/structure-of-the-earth/
Follow along with National Geographic Kids as they journey to the center of Earth.

INDEX